SIFTING THROUGH the ASHES

Wayne William Snellgrove
Fishing Lake First Nation

BLUE FORTUNE ENTERPRISES LLC

SIFTING THROUGH THE ASHES

For information contact :
Blue Fortune Enterprises, LLC
Aster Press
P.O. Box 554
Yorktown, VA 23690
http://blue-fortune.com

Cover design by Blue Fortune Enterprises, LLC

ISBN: 978-1-961548-00-8

First Edition: October 2023

Dedication

This book is dedicated to the ancestors from all nations, tribes and circles who helped beautifully guide us.

Dear Reader,

This is the third edition of this series; like the first two, this book is dedicated to further deepening humanity's awareness and connection to all things powerful, both seen and unseen.

Written in short, simple but compelling truths, the Great Spirit offers these meditations and messages to sit within our ceremony of life together.

Let us allow the love of these messages to flow through us and from all nations, circles, and tribes.

"Sifting through the embers and ashes."

The ashes of the fire are the ashes of our sacred ancestors.

MEDITATION 1

We raise our conscious connection with both the seen and unseen by the simple acknowledgement of our ancestors flowing through us.

MEDITATION 2

We are Earth, and Earth is us.
How can we help heal Mother Earth and ourselves without the help of our ancestors and Mother Earth? We absolutely cannot. We must seek aid from both the seen and unseen.

MEDITATION 3

Natural law includes spider web medicine. The web of life. Both seen and unseen. This teaches creativity and connection to all life, physically, emotionally, mentally and spiritually. The web itself does not end at earth's outer atmosphere. It includes the center of the earth to the center of the universe and beyond.

MEDITATION 4

All life lives per sacred law, except humans. We must remember that we are sacred law, harmony, and balance.

MEDITATION 5

We have to be aware of the sickness from those who carry more opinions than prayers.

MEDITATION 6

Everything begins with Spirit—the unseen powers. Unaided judgements versus aided prayers are a choice and humanity's journey. One relies on nothing, while the other relies on connection.

MEDITATION 7

Medicine Wheel teaching:
Mother Earth consistently teaches humanity through our non-human relatives.

MEDITATION 8

The Earth and its stillness have a beautiful vibration that is in sync with our hearts, and the center of the universe ever reminds us of the oneness of the sacred circle.

MEDITATION 9

How do we change spiritually, emotionally, mentally, and physically? We learn the ways of Earth. One prayer at a time. Prayer begins with listening.

MEDITATION 10

The spiritual paradox is that we need great strength to let go of those things that make us weak.

MEDITATION 11

Medicine Wheel teaching:
We have a right to start over whenever we want or need to. We do not have to wait for the next sunrise; we wait only for our next breath.

MEDITATION 12

The wind, water, fire, and earth hear everything our minds say.

MEDITATION 13

Ancestors' gift:
We are born. We are our own beautiful medicine bundle.
We are the culmination of prayers, songs, and lessons given
to us by those who have come before us.

MEDITATION 14

When we are communicating with the spring flowers,
we are communicating with Mother Earth.
When we stand in the summer winds,
we are communicating with Mother Earth.
When we are consuming the cool fall waters,
we are communicating with Mother Earth.
When we are sitting by the warm winter fire,
we are communicating with Mother Earth.

MEDITATION 15

One way to forget your pain is to forget the past. But this is also the same way we forget our wisdom.

MEDITATION 16

The real magic of the supernatural happens
when connecting to Earth.

MEDITATION 17

Let us gently keep this in mind:
Spiritual connection isn't a race. It is found in the movement, in both the journey and the destination at the same time.

MEDITATION 18

Our bodies are home to our personal Spirit, and as such, we remember our spirit comes from the lives, power, and wisdom of all our ancestors who reside within us. Hence, we are never truly alone or disconnected from those who love us.

MEDITATION 19

Religion needs scholars and interpretation.
Natural Law does not, because the truth requires no interpretation. If it does not come from the Earth, it is not natural law, it is not the truth.

MEDITATION 20

The ancient ones told us we are a part of all creation. And all creation is a part of us. This means all life is also a part of our same consciousness. This is Natural Law.
We are to live this prayer.

MEDITATION 21

The Medicine Wheel teaches us to always remember the East direction. Our child within. Our first cycle of life. We should be mindful that everything we pray, as well as all of our actions, are heard and seen by our little hands, ears, and hearts walking within us.

MEDITATION 22

Trauma places fire upon our hands, hearts, and eyes, making it difficult to hold on to anything, keep anything in our hearts, and see or connect to those things that are good.

MEDITATION 23

Natural Law:
The language and love of the unseen connect us all.

MEDITATION 24

Earth is our freedom. Earth is living. Earth is oneness. Earth is a living prayer. Earth is our ancestor. Earth is our culture. Earth is our home.

MEDITATION 25

Untouched, unnoticed, unchallenged, and unchecked trauma is the rapacious predator that will eventually take everything from us. The Medicine Wheel tells us we must engage in our darkness. Day and night. We must remember that light medicine guides us back into life.

MEDITATION 26

Lessons from our ancestors and elders say our Creator is with us all the time. Day and night. In sickness and in health. Winter, summer, fall, and spring.

MEDITATION 27

Humanity versus Humility

There are no tests, but there is free will, and choice. Either we choose natural law or we don't.

MEDITATION 28

The masterpiece that is life is already within us. The Earth, the Stars, the Universe. Both seen and unseen. A beautiful gift from those who came before us, our ancestors.

MEDITATION 29

Sacred law:

When we offer tobacco for safe passage throughout the day for others, we in turn offer safe passage to ourselves. We are all related.

MEDITATION 30

Bird medicine:
Our indigenous ancestors understand that bird songs create a frequency and vibration that allow plants to grow and be nourished. The question is, what are we doing with our own sacred voice to nourish others?

MEDITATION 31

Tribes helping tribes means more than two-legged helping two-legged. It means we help all nations, tribes, and circles. The standing nations, the winged, four-legged, creepy crawlies, and other nations.

MEDITATION 32

Everything we offer—words, actions, reactions, and responses—is a reflection of the fire we carry within. How is your light shining?

MEDITATION 33

Trauma changes us emotionally, physically, mentally, and spiritually. Love changes us emotionally, physically, mentally, and spiritually. Anger changes us emotionally, physically, mentally, and spiritually. Happiness changes us emotionally, physically, mentally, and spiritually.

MEDITATION 34

All animals, like humans, always leave their medicine in their wake. Both seen and unseen. The medicine acts as homing beacons, drawing humanity closer to the Creator.
Songs to help us listen to Mother Earth, prayers to help us remember Mother Earth.

MEDITATION 35

Medicine Wheel teaching:
Healing is always ongoing because our trauma and abuse cycles, unless healed, are still changing us in ways that don't serve our highest good.

MEDITATION 36

Be the love that doesn't demand you to be right. Be the love that is always gentle. Be the love that offers and shares peace. Be the love that connects us to all life.

MEDITATION 37

Realigning ourselves in accordance with spiritual law means we are safe and able to understand, create, and honor new boundaries.

MEDITATION 38

Medicine Wheel teaching:
The journey is love, and learning how to make good relations, day or night, rain or shine, summer or winter, is our commitment to Creator.

MEDITATION 39

If our species follows the sacred laws of harmony and balance, the ones offered to us by Mother Earth and our indigenous ancestors, there would be no need for separation, war, or borders.

MEDITATION 40

Natural law:
Where there is gratitude, there is always abundance.

MEDITATION 41

The creator equals and mirrors our clarity emotionally, physically, mentally, and spiritually. When we build a good relationship with the Creator, these will come in abundance.

MEDITATION 42

The Medicine Wheel teaches that a new beginning isn't necessarily only a physical place but a spiritual, emotional, or mental mindset. It can begin with our next breath, anywhere, at any time.

MEDITATION 43

The old ones say:
if you have a desire to know someone, watch them.

MEDITATION 44

It's neither the journey nor the destination that truly matters; it is the company seen and unseen that we help along the way.

MEDITATION 45

Walking this Earth isn't done with the feet
but with the heart.

MEDITATION 46

East Medicine: New beginnings.
When we begin with prayer, we begin with Spirit.
Without this, we do not begin.

MEDITATION 47

Language, specifically of our indigenous ancestors, is not words. They are doorways to other, more powerful, unseen doors like love, understanding, forgiveness, and connection, to and from every direction. Proving once again that our ancestors had it right. We are connected.

MEDITATION 48

Mother Earth does not have or play favorites. Or choose who is good or bad. She only responds to alignment with her sacred laws.

MEDITATION 49

Spiritual growth is a basic and simple understanding that we are always moving into a great version of ourselves. Moving ever closer to our sacred center. That place where harmony and balance live.

MEDITATION 50

Aligning and walking with Mother Earth's spiritual laws reveals our value, purpose, and gifts.

MEDITATION 51

Rainbow prophecy is medicine offered to us by our Indigenous Elders to remind us to welcome all colors and life back into the sacred hoop.

MEDITATION 52

This single spiritual law is one of humanity's forgotten ceremonies. If it's not worth sharing, it's not worth having.

MEDITATION 53

Spiritual awareness:
Becoming aligned with Spiritual law does not include opinions, gossip, or judgment like speaking ill of each other. These are the attributes of those who are sleeping.

MEDITATION 54

Humility robs us of selfishness.

MEDITATION 55

Natural Law is the Great Spirit. Its voice lives and breathes, both seen and unseen. This is consciousness, and its voice lived in our ancestors, through song, ceremony, and dance. Now this voice lives within us. We are all related.

MEDITATION 56

The only currency in this world is a conscious connection to Natural Law.

MEDITATION 57

Natural law:
As we grow spiritually, so does humanity's understanding expand consciousness to all things beautiful and powerful, all life.

MEDITATION 58

Humility medicine question:
The Universe is 13.7 billion years.
Our species is around 300,000 years old. How much do we know and understand about who we are, what we are, and our relationship to all things?

MEDITATION 59

As the people of Turtle Island, we tell our traditional stories for many reasons. The first is to teach our children about our relationship and connection to our Mother Earth. The deeper teaching is imagination. Stories involve endlessly listening to our imagination. The old ones say if we lose our connection with Mother Earth, we will lose our connection to our imagination. If we lose our imagination, we not only begin to lose our future but also lose sight of the next seven generations. We will spiral into calamity, crisis, and chaos.

MEDITATION 60

Natural Law:
Those who see the light most are the ones who share the light most.

MEDITATION 61

Love. One of the Seven Sacred Teachings.
Humility, truth, strength, respect, honesty, and wisdom.
It isn't separate from the other teachings; it is all-inclusive.
It is who we are. Hence, Love isn't everything, it's the only thing. It is our connection to life. To Mother Earth.
And all her creation.

MEDITATION 62

Eagle and Hawk Medicine:
Our eyes are powerful Medicine, not only to view beautiful physical medicine but with the assistance of our ancestors, to see the unseen. Emotionally, mentally, and spiritually.

MEDITATION 63

When our ancestors state our spiritual job, "Create good relations to all things beautiful," they are referring to all the things the Great Spirit has made. Not only our two-legged nations, circles, and tribes. But all nations, circles, and tribes. We must begin by sitting and listening to them. Hearing their stories and wisdom. Understanding their ancestors and their future seven generations. Both seen and unseen. Physically and spiritually. Only then will we begin to understand the value in this world and the next.

MEDITATION 64

Love is not male or female. Like the Great Spirit, love does not need either but can create both. Neither love nor the Great Spirit can be divided, lessened, or defeated. It is the power that doesn't respond to size or depend on size.

MEDITATION 65

The old one says we must take time to look up at the stars. They're their own beautiful, sacred direction.
We must listen to them, like Mother Earth. They have a pearl of unique wisdom and teaching all their own. If we are to evolve as a species, we learn to communicate with them in this beautiful way.

MEDITATION 66

Courage doesn't have to be loud and aggressive.
Courage can be that little voice that says keep going.

MEDITATION 67

Spiritual law:
The mind will replay what the heart has not learned.

MEDITATION 68

Spiritual law:
What happens in the physical world is mirrored in the Spirit world. Our ecosystem is a beautiful medicine. Environments create weather, such as the rainforest or desert. The weather depends on what's happening around them, the spiritual neighborhood. This is a mirror of what happens to humanity. What are we surrounding ourselves with? What conversation, people, social media, prayers, lack of prayers, active drug addicts? Fire? Water? Earth? Elders? Wisdom keepers? Singers? Alcohol?
Let us always be mindful of our surroundings.

MEDITATION 69

The truth is always spiritual. Pain is a truth. Pain is often the gateway to healing and wisdom — the touchstone to growth and clarity. When unchecked and unattended, it is also the gateway to calamity, crisis, and chaos.

MEDITATION 70

Spiritual Law:
The first education is imagination. The last education is imagination. And everything in between is based on imagination.

MEDITATION 71

Medicine Wheel:
Our physical connection to Earth is our unseen connection to Spirit.

MEDITATION 72

Everything is ceremony. Every word and thought is a singular ceremony, a part of the ceremony of life.

MEDITATION 73

Our spoken language is supposed to mirror our connection to the world around us, to empower us.

MEDITATION 74

Medicine Wheel teaching:
Clarity's gift is understanding we can share Creator's love.

MEDITATION 75

The Elder says our breath carries more than words. We create what we offer verbally. It carries our future and the future of the next seven generations.

MEDITATION 76

Every day, we continually walk in, through, and out of both seen and unseen worlds.

MEDITATION 77

We lay down and offer what no longer serves us or life. We let go of our anger, sadness, and loneliness by placing them in our heart, transmuting them to love, and offering them back to the Creator.

MEDITATION 78

Spiritual growth question:
Are we ready to accept, love, and honor a better version of ourselves?

MEDITATION 79

Love. One of the seven sacred teachings, represented by the Eagle, who has always been the messenger of the Great Spirit. Our lives and how we live are our messages to the world.

MEDITATION 80

The narrative of right and wrong is a colonial narrative. This isn't in alignment with Natural Law. Mother Earth doesn't use this spiritual language, so we should follow suit. Everything begins with a connection. Connection to the language of Mother Earth, the sounds she uses to communicate with us.

MEDITATION 81

Mother Earth teaches us that our diversity is our beauty. Our beauty teaches connection to one another. Our connection brings us closer to our Creator.

MEDITATION 82

We are the rain and spaces in between. We are the sun's rays and the spaces in between. We are the Earth and the spaces in between. We are the wind and air and the spaces in between. We are all connected.

MEDITATION 83

Personal self-care includes how we speak, listen, and relate to Mother Earth.

MEDITATION 84

If we do not have any room for spiritual transparency or
personal vulnerability, we have no room for
growth or wisdom.
The choice is ours.

MEDITATION 85

Brave. One of the seven sacred teachings presented to us by the bear. One that guides us back into life. It gives us strength to face our greatest enemy ourselves. Brave offers our prayers a safe place as we protect the prayers that protect us. Strength says it may be in the next prayer that changes our destiny.

MEDITATION 86

How we pray to the water and Mother Earth depends on how well we understand and communicate with the sacred feminine.

MEDITATION 87

Choice.
Good or bad, better or worse, right or wrong are the only alternatives left if we ignore our connection to Mother Earth and the Great Spirit.

MEDITATION 88

Humanity's uniqueness is a direct reflection of Mother Earth.

MEDITATION 89

Without a connection with our sacred center, we will live on the peripheries of life, living and breathing within the illusionary walls of loneliness, sadness, fear, and anger.

MEDITATION 90

Energy isn't all physical. It is also emotional and mental. And it isn't about power or strength but connection and connection to consciousness.

MEDITATION 91

Let us learn to smile at the rising sun. When we understand this, we understand we are smiling at our new beginnings. We smile at the return of our ancestors. We are smiling at another day of life.

MEDITATION 92

We search the ends of the Earth until we find our place in it.
And then we discover we are the Earth all along.

MEDITATION 93

Sound is a gift from the Creator. Language is sound that unlocks different places, feelings, and dimensions. We know music and songs bring us to a different place, closer to our Creator. Medicine for Spirit. Medicine for all: children, youth, adults, and elders.

MEDITATION 94

As Indigenous, language is our direct connection to Creator. It is used to supplement and extend communication from our hearts and build good relations with all tribes, circles, and nations. It carries the resonance and energy of the heart.

MEDITATION 95

We are all empathetic. We are all Mother Earth. The two are forever linked. Our empathic abilities are directly based on our connection to Mother Earth. This is a gift from the Creator. As we grow spiritually and connect to Mother Earth and all her medicines, empaths feel the meaning behind the words and languages, both spoken and unspoken.

MEDITATION 96

Indigenous language begins with an intention that creates energy with sounds and, in the end, creates a beautiful connection to life.

MEDITATION 97

If we do not live the way of Earth, it may not be us who suffer, but it will definitely be our children and our children's children.

MEDITATION 98

Energy isn't always physical, it is also emotional, mental, and spiritual. Energy isn't about power or strength but connection.

MEDITATION 99

Humanity:
Change isn't hard, resistance to it is. Be the flow of the seasons, one season doesn't resist the other.

MEDITATION 100

Our inside garden is where life begins to flow.

MEDITATION 101

If we are Earth, there is a clear difference between living with her and living on her.

MEDITATION 102

The ancient ones and the elders say we all have value for our communities. None of us are useless in Creator's Spiritual economy. The journey is called the Red Road, the road of wellness, pointing us close to our sacred center. The closer we are to our sacred center, the more value we place on our place in the circle, the circle of life.

MEDITATION 103

If our spiritual life does not include a relationship with Mother Earth, then it is incomplete.

MEDITATION 104

Mother Earth Medicine:
If we ignore the songs and voices from Mother Earth, it isn't Mother who suffers, it will most likely be the next seven generations.

MEDITATION 105

Sunrise medicine shines upon the return of our ancestors.

MEDITATION 106

Empath and compassion have a rhythm, harmony, and a language we'll know little about if we do not align ourselves with natural law.

MEDITATION 107

The natural law of humility states we consistently seek. We consult and commune with those nations, circles, and tribes, especially those nations, circles, and tribes that live the way of natural law.

MEDITATION 108

Circle Medicine:
Part of our journey is to help each other find the sacred gifts given to us by the Creator. After we find them, our job is to share our gifts with all nations, circles, and tribes.

MEDITATION 109

Remember, we are the gift to the next seven generations from our ancestors. Let us pray and walk accordingly.

MEDITATION 110

We share a heartbeat with Mother Earth and all her life.

MEDITATION 111

If it's an attack on any part of our human circle, it's an attack against Mother Earth.
What happens to us, happens to Mother Earth.
What happens to Mother Earth, happens to us.

MEDITATION 112

We are here not because of our darkness but because of the light we are and carry.

MEDITATION 113

The sacred listening journey: We pray to listen to a thousand different voices of our ancestors.

MEDITATION 114

Language, culture, and heritage mean very little when we all sit together with love in our hearts for each other.

MEDITATION 115

We have to teach our children that the supernatural is natural, and the natural is the magic of Mother Earth.

MEDITATION 116

Medicine Wheel teaching, Turtle Medicine:
The medicine of truth is natural law. It doesn't negotiate. The truth is never decisive. Our resistance to it is — emotionally, mentally, spiritually, and physically.

MEDITATION 117

Prayers and Mother Earth:
The Earth without imagination is dead. The Earth with imagination comes alive. That is why we, as Indigenous, tell stories of little animals such as grandmother mole bringing life to the underground. The seeds tell us that we can grow in dark places. Grandpa Oak tells us how important it is to stay grounded.

MEDITATION 118

When we seek out our healing, our healing has already begun.

MEDITATION 119

Medicine Wheel teaching:
We can not find or go home until we find our truth. Our truth is home.

MEDITATION 120

Our indigenous language is our place of healing. Our seven sacred elements of language are humility, love, truth, courage, respect, honesty, and wisdom.

MEDITATION 121

Medicine Wheel teaching:
Being all in: It is difficult to be present, spiritually, emotionally, mentally, and physically when we do not have Creator's presence in our lives.

MEDITATION 122

Love never uses fear to control. It never threatens or manipulates. Using fear to control isn't love, it is something else.

MEDITATION 123

Medicine Wheel teaching is understanding Children's wisdom are some of the most powerful teachings. Without listening, we will never understand our own child within us.

MEDITATION 124

Medicine Wheel teaching:
If you can't share it, don't take it.

MEDITATION 125

Medicine wheel teaching:
We offer tobacco for many reasons. The main reason is offering. When we ask, we always offer tobacco. Without offering, we can not ask. Offering tobacco opens the spiritual door.

MEDITATION 126

Our first vision is imagination because we do not need our eyes. To see a better life, a life change, we can use our sightless vision to create whatever we want. Our connection to life is our vision. We must never grow out of looking at and honoring our imagination.

MEDITATION 127

The Great Spirit is sometimes referred to as The Great Mystery. In some strange and beautiful way, we chose our journey. We have chosen life. Now we have the opportunity to choose the course of our lives with the prayers we choose to walk with or without.

MEDITATION 128

Humanity's journey is learning to transmute everything into love and light. From every breath, situation, and up to and including our entire life.

MEDITATION 129

Our traditional Indigenous ways haven't been lost, like the sun, the moon, and the Earth have never left. They are the wisdom keepers. Keepers of the sacred fire at the center of the Universe. We must remember they are there and learn to make good relations again. They are waiting for us. If we do not live these ways, the teachings won't die—we will.

MEDITATION 130

The ceremony, journey, and destination.
In honoring Mother Earth, we are reminded that we are Mother Earth.

MEDITATION 131

Understanding the flow, patience, and prayer. Allow time for the Earth medicines to speak to you. Be patient. Be aware. And listen.

MEDITATION 132

Humans write holy books. Mother Earth creates life, you, and the universe.

MEDITATION 133

Medicine Wheel and the Seven Sacred Teachings: Transition, transmute, transforms. In the beginning, it is a change in perception. It's not what happens to us, it's how we look at it.

MEDITATION 134

Our connections to Mother Earth and the Great Spirit haven't gone anywhere—humanity has walked away. We have to walk back; the ancestors know the way.

MEDITATION 135

The quickest way to kill our serenity is to compare it to someone else's.

MEDITATION 136

Animals, plants, winged nations, fish nations, Earth, and all
her elements should have equal rights,
just like humans should.

MEDITATION 137

One of the worst epidemics isn't physical at all, it's spiritual — humanity's inability to feel the love and connection to Mother Earth. Humanity is grieving, mourning the loss of our mother directly below our feet.

MEDITATION 138

When we change the spiritual things within us, we change the physical things we see around us.

MEDITATION 139

Spiritual Silence:
Silence doesn't mean lack of noise, it means it does not disturb our own sacred serenity.

MEDITATION 140

Humor medicine:
Humor is necessary for our spiritual development. It is one of our most forgotten ceremonies.
We are all behind on our laughter.

MEDITATION 141

Discernment medicine:
Seek the knowledge of all spiritual paths but find and walk with the one that honors all others.

MEDICINE 142

Mother Nature's law of harmony and balance will always restore and bring life to a lifeless place. That place of sadness, loneliness, and despair within all of us.

MEDICINE 143

We are born a thousand times to remember the dreams, smiles, and laughter of one child. Often that child is us. Other times, it is our ancestors.

MEDITATION 144

Sacred law states we don't have to understand something to respect it. We don't have to like it to accept it. It doesn't have to make sense for us to love it. Sometimes, we just have to accept life's mysteries. This is the Great Mystery. This is the Great journey within.

MEDITATION 145

For living the prayer of harmony and balance, we must offer our gifts and share them with the world.

MEDITATION 146

Mother Earth:
We will find peace when connected to those medicines that live in peace.

MEDIATION 147

Sacred law of life:
We awaken what we think. What we think, we create. This is the fusion of prayer and imagination and our spiritual and physical manifestations. This creates life.

MEDITATION 148

If we want peace on Earth, we must connect to Earth.

MEDITATION 149

Knowledge is knowing silence is silent. Wisdom is knowing silence is never silent.

MEDITATION 150

We are Earth. We come from all life. We are supposed to pray for all life. We are supposed to help all life. We are supposed to pray with all life. Only then will we realize we are a part of all life.

MEDITATION 151

Seven sacred directions equals the Seven sacred teachings. When we pray with and for all other relatives, this opens the unseen door to let the power flow in from all directions. must sit in the light to feel the darkness.

MEDITATION 152

Keeping healthy boundaries is loving ourselves. If we don't, we don't think less of those who we allowed to violate our boundaries. We think less of ourselves.

MEDITATION 153

Natural Law:
Understanding the sacred. Silence and stillness are languages that never stop speaking.

MEDITATION 154

Mother Earth and our ancestors hold the secrets of life, love, and light. The only way we can find, hear, and understand them is when we offer prayers of life, love, and light to others and the next seven generations.

MEDITATION 155

Religion is man's fatal distraction. Replacing the patriarchal alignment with honoring the sacred lifegivers.
Only Mother Earth can return harmony and balance.

MEDITATION 156

The paradox is we must sit in the darkness to feel the light. We must sit in the light to feel the darkness.

MEDITATION 157

Spirituality 101:
When we begin to listen to and look at Mother Earth, we begin to notice her medicine is already within us.

MEDITATION 158

Looking back:
The past medicine is a beautiful place to remember the strength and courage we've gained from our struggles.

MEDITATION 159

We are traveling on beautiful journeys. Remember often, we are not in the same seasons; some are winter, a time for reflection. Others may be in a new beginning, spring. And still others in the fall. Be gentle with each other because we often don't know what season someone is traveling through.

MEDITATION 160

We are not only the Sun. We are not only the rain. We are not only the darkness and the light. We are not only the seasons. We are everything. We are all related.

MEDITATION 161

Those not in good relation with their truth will not be loyal to yours.

MEDITATION 162

It's easy to love our light, but can we love our darkness?

MEDITATION 163

Natural Law:
Those who fail to live the truth are destined to repeat the failure.

MEDITATION 164

We are here to honor, love, and make good relations to all things beautiful, including ourselves.

MEDITATION 165

We destroy land if we are not connected to her. We destroy ourselves if we are not connected to her. We are all related.

MEDITATION 166

The Creator's first prayer for us was offering us life. Our first prayer should be gratitude for our life. To sustain our life, our second prayer should be for all life and offering prayers for those who came before us, our ancestors. To round out our prayers, we should offer all to the next seven generations.

MEDITATION 167

Buffalo Medicine. Respect:
One of the seven sacred teachings. Connection to this prayer is an acknowledgment of all life. We have an equal relationship with all nations, circles, and tribes. Like breath, respect is our birthright. Offering respect is offering life, especially to those who fail to offer it to us.

MEDITATION 168

For those who choose to walk the Red Road, we understand how to walk the way of The Great Spirit of Natural Law. The first agreement with the great spirit is the agreement, "We mean no harm in what we do."

MEDITATION 169

Our expression of life includes our right to be happy and laugh. We must never forget how to smile. We never fail to express our happy medicine.

MEDITATION 170

Healing ceremony:
The saddest story isn't the one we haven't heard, it's the one inside us that we can't tell.

MEDITATION 171

We, as humans, create and hold on to our sickness. Trauma. We are told to get over it. We feel separated from everything. *Animals are stupid. Money is power. My only relations are human and blood family. My God has a higher sanction. I have to beg for everything from my religion. Religion is punishing me. My political side is right. Oneness is sameness. Only humans know God. I'm better than you. Earth is only a resource. God hates gays. We are the chosen people. My trauma doesn't affect me. My messiah is better than your savior. I'm winning. I lost. My investment portfolio is more critical than me wasting time praying for my enemies. I kill my enemies. It's crucial I'm always right. I pray for only what I need. My religion is better than yours. It would be best if you believed what I believe. My God has a higher sanction over all your Gods.*

These are the spiritual illnesses that will keep us sick.

MEDITATION 172

Creator created all of us to learn and live by Spiritual Law with all life. This Law is designed to create a beautiful Earth and universe.

MEDITATION 173

Remembering, "We are Mother Earth" is the beginning of our healing. It reminds us we are part of a beautiful, larger whole, both seen and unseen.

MEDITATION 174

Until we remember we are Earth, we will always try to be somewhere and someone else. Emotionally, spiritually, mentally, and physically.

MEDITATION 175

Helping others must be a part of our daily prayers. Without it, our prayers are incomplete.

MEDITATION 176

As we grow, so does the healing of the ancestors behind us and the seven generations before us. We are all related, seen and unseen.

MEDITATION 177

Mother Earth is our heritage. She is our responsibility. And to those who walked in her spiritual footsteps, we are a beautiful extension of our ancestors. We are to honor all to find ourselves.

MEDITATION 178

A colonial sickness: When imagination is taken away either spiritually, emotionally, or mentally, it is called indoctrination. This defines and maintains the illusion, "Oneness is sameness." This is the definition of colonial religion.

MEDITATION 179

We are our ancestor's keepers—guardians of the prayers they have offered us. We are only the keepers of the flames until it is time for us to transition into the next world.

MEDITATION 180

We all have beautiful gifts given and offered to us by the Creator and those who came before us. These gifts can only be realized by our direct relationships with our sacred Mother Earth.

MEDITATION 181

When we remember we are Earth, we remember our ancestors. When we remember our ancestors, we remember our healing. When we remember our healing, we remember we are Spirit. When we remember our Spirit, the door to magic and miracles opens.

MEDITATION 182

As Indigenous people, we understand that the content of our characters begins with and is based upon our relationship with the seven sacred teachings and Mother Earth.

MEDITATION 183

Our indigenous language is the great secret to connecting to healing, which is Mother Earth.

MEDITATION 184

True love among humanity will never happen until we realize we are all brothers and sisters.

MEDITATION 185

Medicine Wheel teaching:
Earth isn't separate from our humanity. Without it, we will never understand our humanity.

MEDITATION 186

Colonial versus Spiritual:
Knowledge isn't power. Mother Earth is. Only through the connection to and application of Mother Earth's medicine is wisdom and healing gained and alignment restored.

MEDITATION 187

Listening is spiritual education and humility wrapped into one. Without it, we have little imagination and vision.

MEDITATION 188

Spiritual education:
We do what we need to do until we can
make a better decision.

MEDITATION 189

Spiritual synchronization isn't by chance or luck. It is pure alignment with natural law. Often, we do not understand the simplicity of this universal agreement. Happiness is the alignment and reflection of this spiritual law.

MEDITATION 190

The difference between wisdom and knowledge:
one gives advice, the other offers experience.

MEDITATION 191

The old one says water holds and carries the prayers of our ancestors. We can talk to them directly and ask for healing with every drop we drink.

MEDITATION 192

The medicine is all related and beautifully offered to us. Sight is given to us by our ancestors. Love is given to us by the land. Strength is given to us by the next seven generations.

MEDITATION 193

Light, love, and life are all variations of the same thing. One can not have one without the others.

MEDITATION 194

We are children of the universe. We could live 1,000 lifetimes learning about Mother Earth and still only know a little.

MEDITATION 195

If we are not encouraging others daily, why not?

MEDITATION 196

If we have established that we are Earth and Earth is us, then our connection to Earth has to be an integral part of self-love, healing, and recovery. If it is not, it is incomplete.

MEDITATION 197

Our prayers cannot be heard if we do not verbally say them aloud. We must verbalize everything, because this is our intent to both worlds, seen and unseen.

MEDITATION 198

Many of us have years of colonial education but no education on how to honor, love, and respect Mother Earth.

MEDITATION 199

Peace can come in many forms, emotionally, mentally, physically, and spiritually. Welcome these relatives at any time. For peace, do not make mistakes or arrive at the wrong time. It comes because you offer, pray, and prepare.

MEDITATION 200

The sky direction includes the father sky cloud nations, thunder beings, and Star Nations. All have intimate relations with and are a part of humanity just as the trees, the water, winged nations, fish nations and seasons and all other nations' circles and tribes.

MEDITATION 201

Humanity's choice:
Love consciously or live unconsciously.

MEDITATION 202

Humanity's prayer: journey and destination. Earth first, or we will lose everything.

MEDITATION 203

The land speaks to those who listen.

MEDITATION 204

Spiritual progress begins when we start with gratitude and offerings.

MEDITATION 205

Those who bring up the past to poison you still have unhealed poison in themselves.

MEDITATION 206

The Great Spirit consistently teaches us on all levels: emotionally, mentally, physically, and spiritually. Is humanity ready to acknowledge, accept, and learn these teachings?

MEDITATION 207

In some strange, beautiful, and mysterious way, we are a part of everything beautiful — the sunsets, the incoming tide, the songs of the spring, the aurora borealis, every snowflake, the mountain lion, hummingbird — everything.

MEDITATION 208

Love is an emotion. Love is a feeling. But love is also what we do.

MEDITATION 209

Every heartbeat is a gift and living prayer from a million-million ancestors. We are to hold this gift, honor, love, and protect it until the time to offer it to the next generation.

MEDITATION 210

We are as much a part of the stars as the Earth. As above and as below, both seen and unseen. We are all related.

MEDITATION 211

We live in a world where our thoughts create our environment, not only physically but emotionally, mentally, and spiritually. This is natural law.

MEDITATION 212

Humanity has always had two choices: move toward or away from the sacred laws of Earth.

MEDITATION 213

In many of our ancient indigenous stories of creation, Mother Earth said, "All we have is each other."

MEDITATION 214

On Mother Earth, every single life since the beginning of creation, every nation, circle, and tribe, is our ancestor.

MEDITATION 215

Love, light, and life. Like energy, they can never be destroyed. Only forms to transmute into, through and out of different forms. Humanity will keep evolving into, through, and out of various life forms, both seen and unseen.

MEDITATION 216

Being empathic is not a disease. We all experience and live in a feeling universe. We are given five senses to observe and make good relations to these feelings. To an empath, these can be confusing because we live in two worlds, Mother Earth realms and the colonial. Let's not confuse one with the other, the chaos, calamity and crisis of the colonial and the natural rhythms and harmony offered to us by Mother Earth. We are supposed to live in harmony and happiness.

MEDITATION 217

We are natural law. Earth is natural law. Eagles are natural law. Sunrise is natural law. Star nations are natural law. The moon is natural law. The Turtle is natural law. The ancestors are natural law. Our dreams are natural law.

MEDITATION 218

Let our prayers of love, life, and light be invincible today.

MEDITATION 219

The path of peace begins at the center of the universe, in the first fire that ever was. It rode the backs of the thunder beings straight into our Mother's wombs and entered our hearts. There we must look after it, nurture it, love it, and protect it from enemies internal and external.

MEDITATION 220

One of the highest forms of wisdom is the ability to listen without judgment.

MEDITATION 221

The path of harmony and balance. The hate offered us by the colonial world has to be matched by our connection to love what we've been offered by Mother Earth.

MEDITATION 222

It is a beautiful sign of the wisdom of harmony and balance when we can share tears of sadness and joy.

MEDITATION 223

Like the Turtle, the truth does not negotiate emotionally, spiritually, mentally, or physically. It just is, like the seasons.

MEDITATION 224

The sun lights the seen. The moon lights the unseen.

MEDITATION 225

Sacred Law:
We heal at the exact same level we engage in the seven sacred laws offered to us.

MEDITATION 226

Not only will humanity suffer, but our next seven generations will suffer without our prayer and commitment to Unity. Unity is harmony and balance.

MEDITATION 227

Forgotten ceremony. Humanity is held together by the spiritual, mental, emotional, and physical connection we have to our Mother Earth.

MEDITATION 228

Our prayers today feed the next seven generations.

MEDITATION 229

Part of our stories that one day our ancestors will ask us is how well we loved Mother Earth.

MEDITATION 230

What I offer you, I offer to myself. The refusal to pray for our enemies is the prayer and offering we give our children. We pass along this sickness.

MEDITATION 231

The Standing Nations already know intimately the sound and rhythm of our heartbeat.

MEDITATION 232

How we walk on Mother Earth represents our relationship with her. Walk gently. Pray gently. Offer gently. Connect gently.

MEDITATION 233

We are not only the sons and daughters of Mother Earth but also of the Universe.

MEDITATION 234

Spirituality 101:
The first medicine of life is understanding we are a part of all life. This is a living prayer and journey to connect to everything that gives us life.

MEDITATION 235

Understanding the true spiritual flow. Water in the ocean, rivers, and lakes all intimately hears and understands the sacred water flowing through our bodies. To come full circle, are we listening and connecting to the flowing water around us? Water is life.

MEDITATION 236

Truth. The only true wealth and abundance is creating a better world for the next seven generations.

MEDITATION 237

Who we are as a culture and as individuals is a clear history of the prayers we carry.

MEDITATION 238

Medicine Wheel teaching:
All life speaks. All life has a voice. All life has a language. But not all languages are spoken. To speak for the voiceless, like the Standing Nations, we must connect to the heartbeat of all nations.

MEDITATION 239

Humans, Unity, and the Medicine Wheel teaching:
Humans standing together is only the beginning of unity.
But until we learn to stand together with all of Mother
Earth's life, we will never understand unity.

MEDITATION 240

Natural Law:
If we never look for it in our hearts, we will never see it with our eyes.

MEDITATION 241

Connecting to Mother Earth is self-care. Self-care is self-love. Self-love is never selfish.

MEDITATION 242

Earth is humanity. We will never understand ourselves until we understand our relationship with Mother Earth. Earth is a way of life; she is a living, breathing, walking long prayer.

MEDITATION 243

The land speaks to all of us. She has never stopped speaking to us. Are we listening? Do we know what to listen for? She talks to us emotionally, mentally, spiritually, and physically.

MEDITATION 244

Sunrise Medicine:
When we gaze into the eyes of the sunrise, we gaze into the eyes of the Great Spirit and all our ancestors.

MEDITATION 245

Full circle:
We come from a place of prayers, our ancestors, and now we are the physical guardians of the prayers that gave us life. We must protect these prayers of life for the next seven generations.

MEDITATION 246

Silence is a language, and when understood and used effectively, it is the only language that can listen and speak at the same time.

MEDITATION 247

The change we want to see in this world is found in the prayers we walk with.

MEDITATION 248

Philosophy of Peace:
Mother Earth has never started or waged war. One season does not resist or fight the previous. The night does not fight the sunrise. Humanity has forgotten we are not at war. We are to transition smoothly from one moment to the next.

MEDITATION 249

Natural Law:
Nothing is wasted in Mother Earth's spiritual economy. Every tear of sadness is turned into life. Every emotional sorrow is turned back into life. All the wildfire ashes are the return of life to our future ancestors.

MEDITATION 250

Prayer is the sunlight we always carry. This is the same sunlight that has been offered to us by our ancestors. And we are to carry this for the next seven generations.

MEDITATION 251

The seven sacred laws of love, humility, honesty, truth, respect, courage, and wisdom, when followed, will lead humanity to one consciousness.

MEDITATION 252

The great and sacred law of humility cannot be broken, splintered, or negotiated with, beginning with we are Earth. This is the law of the land. What we do to Earth, we do to ourselves. If we fail to protect Earth, we fail to protect ourselves. No religion, God, or holy book has a higher sanction over Mother Earth.

MEDITATION 253

Natural law:
All things mirror each other, seen and unseen. Just as the sage cleans the air of impurities, it cleans unseen realms of negative energy. Science has proved humans can only see a small percentage of the light spectrum, and we can only hear only specific frequencies. This tells us that there is so much we don't know or even understand, let alone connected to in the spirit world.

MEDITATION 254

Children and the Medicine Wheel:
It not only takes a whole village to raise a child but a relationship with all of Mother Earth to help teach one child physically, emotionally, mentally and spiritually. All seasons, plants, animals, creepy crawlies, all the elements, stars and star nations have medicine to help assist, teach, and raise one child. Even the ancestors, as well as the future generations, have beautiful and powerful teachings for our children.

MEDITATION 255

Truth and the Turtle:
The truth is we are Earth. Whether we understand this or not. All our relationships with Mother Earth are based on this truth. However, our human perception is often based on something else. Religion. Right or wrong. Better or worse. Rarely are our prayers and perception aligned with this truth. Those who were aligned, like our Indigenous ancestors, lived a very different life. Their historical relationship isn't something that needs to be studied but lived.

MEDITATION 256

Medicine Wheel teaching:
Every teaching has a more profound connection that reaches far beyond the stars. The spiritual paradox is that to be able to see this place beyond the beyond, humanity must connect to those medicines right in front of us.

MEDITATION 257

Listening isn't listening until we use all five senses. Vision isn't vision until we use all five senses. Smell isn't smell until we use all five senses. Touch isn't touch until we use all five senses. Taste isn't taste until we use all five senses.

MEDITATION 258

Circle Medicine:
The circle is equality. For equality to be represented in society, humanity must relinquish its thirst for patriarchal establishments as well as begin to incorporate Mother Earth in all our decisions.

MEDITATION 259

Medicine Wheel teaching:
Our children, like the Earth and all her medicines, are only loaned to us.

MEDITATION 260

Observation Medicine:
We are the prayers we carry when no one is looking.

MEDITATION 261

Gratitude Medicine:
Without starting our day with gratitude, it leaves a void. Left unchecked, this void leads to the spiritual disease of entitlement, which leads to sadness, loneliness, and depression.

MEDITATION 262

Like the braid of sweetgrass, Mother Earth, the ancestors, humanity, and the future seven generations are forever intertwined and overlapping.

MEDITATION 263

Sacred listening:
When properly spoken, listening has a voice that can speak and hear at the same time.

MEDITATION 264

Sky medicine, Star Nation relatives:
The old ones say the Star nations are a part of us and are a part of Mother Earth's physical and spiritual landscape, both seen and unseen.

MEDITATION 265

Medicine Teaching:
All nations have seventh-generation prayers. It isn't only a human prayer. It is a living prayer. We are all related.

MEDITATION 266

Mother Earth = ME

MEDITATION 267

Prayers that do not include Mother Earth are incomplete.
Prayers that do not include our ancestors are incomplete.
Prayers that do not include our next seven
generations are incomplete.

MEDITATION 268

Natural law of Collective Consciousness:
We understand that humanity is all related. But let's not forget the visions and prophecies from all nations, tribes, and circles are all related. Brought together and included by our collective consciousness.

MEDITATION 269

Obeying our enemy is keeping the anger, resentment, and fear. We must learn to allow love, healing, and releasing our enemies through prayer and ceremony.

MEDITATION 270

Let us pray collectively for the courage and strength to protect Mother Earth and all her sacredness.

MEDITATION 271

Our ancestors knew there was healing in sound. They watched closely interconnected relationships between songbirds singing and the flowers blooming. Imagine if our species spoke kindly to each other. What world could we offer to the next seven generations?

MEDITATION 272

A religion doesn't measure spirituality, just as educational degrees do not measure intelligence and age doesn't measure maturity.

MEDITATION 273

Truth: The more truth we carry, the lighter the load.
Humility: The more humility we carry, the lighter the load.
Honesty: The more honesty we carry, the lighter the load.
Respect: The more respect we carry, the lighter the load.
Courage: The more courage we carry, the lighter the load.
Wisdom: The more wisdom we carry, the lighter the load.
Love: The more love we carry, the lighter the load.

MEDITATION 274

Hollow bone medicine is spiritual, emotional, mental, and physical. The common thread to all these aspects has always been a collective conscious connection, the voice of universal health and healing that unites us all.

MEDITATION 275

All our relatives are connected.
How we live our lives will be reflected in the dreams and prayers of the next seven generations.

MEDITATION 276

All the memories of our ancestors reside within us.

MEDITATION 277

Without our connection to Mother Earth, humanity's most endangered species is our next seven generations.

MEDITATION 278

We have zero minorities, only humans.

MEDITATION 279

A gentle shift in consciousness. Remember that we live in a colonial society; it is broken, not us. We can stop living in broken ways and believing in broken prayers. Let us start by living the way of the Earth, and we heal collectively.

MEDITATION 280

Those who refuse to consciously treat Mother Earth as an ally will treat her unconsciously as the enemy.

MEDITATION 281

We are physical. We are spiritual. We are the seen. We are the unseen. We can never be one without the other. We are forever overlapped and intertwined conscious beings.

MEDITATION 282

Medicine Wheel Teaching:
Love without humility is manipulation.

MEDITATION 283

Religion is a choice. Humans are what we are. We are Earth.

MEDITATION 284

Humanity:
We are never so lost that the medicines of Earth cannot restore our humanity.

MEDITATION 285

We are the relationship between the seen and unseen. We must act accordingly. Breath without gratitude isn't enough, just like prayer without action isn't enough.

MEDITATION 286

Circle unity medicine:
The concept of otherness is the seed of genocide.

MEDITATION 287

Standing Nation Medicine:
All trees are related to the first tree, the tree of life. When we feel weak, we can ask the sacred tree for peace, grounding, and strength.

MEDITATION 288

Prayer is our creation, our imagination, ourselves, and our future. We are one.

MEDITATION 289

Sound medicine:
We speak in tones. Tones are frequency. Language is frequency. Frequency is vibrations.
Vibrations connect us to consciousness.

MEDITATION 290

Natural law:
The spiritual void appears if humanity is not grounded with Mother Earth and its sacred laws. Often we will fall for any belief, such as greed, genocide, and patriarchal religion. Nothing can replace natural law.

MEDITATION 291

All are related. If the earth changes, humanity changes. If the Earth dies, humanity dies. If Earth lives, we live.

MEDITATION 292

Water Medicine:
Tears are a language which allows us to see our hearts.

MEDITATION 293

Those who create enemies are already enemies with themselves.

MEDITATION 294

Our voices are strong when our ancestors flow through it.

MEDITATION 295

Our first and forgotten language is consciousness.

MEDITATION 296

Fire:
There is fire from the center of the universe. This is the first fire that represents the original prayer in physical form. This is the fire that gave us life—traveling from the center of the universe to the womb of our Mother. The great spark of life that gave us our heartbeat. This fire, this heart, is our ceremony that tells us how to walk in harmony and balance. We must listen to our hearts to understand the original prayer.

MEDITATION 297

Our human job, with the help of Mother Earth, the ancestors, and the Great Spirit, is to bring harmony and balance back to our hearts. From there, it is to filter out into our family and communities.

MEDITATION 298

The paradox is that we ascend to spiritual realms by grounding physically to Mother Earth.

MEDITATION 299

As indigenous peoples, we understand we are born with beautiful and powerful birth rights not only associated with but intimately connected to the Seven sacred teachings of truth, honesty, wisdom, love, humility, respect, and strength.

MEDITATION 300

The spiritual paradigm is that we grow with every tree we plant and pray with.

MEDITATION 301

Humility is the understanding that we don't know enough to know all.

MEDITATION 302

Flowers do not compare or compete. Spring does not compete with summer. The breeze does not compare itself to the wind.

MEDITATION 303

Mother Earth has songs for us daily. It is sound wisdom to help us through the storms of life.

MEDITATION 304

The Red Road. The road of wellness. At the beginning of our wellness journey, we may not know our ancestors, but they already know us intimately.

MEDITATION 305

Spiritual law. Sacred law. Nobody owns sacred law. To live a good life, we are supposed to be keepers of these laws. Let us not be confused. Sacred laws aren't about being right or wrong or good or bad, but simply about connecting to those principles that offer us life.

MEDITATION 306

Star Nation teaching:
The original prayer at the center of the universe is represented in all the stars in the sky.
We are related to all other stars.

MEDITATION 307

Earth Medicine:
The layers of the Earth also represent the prayer and history of the Earth. Earth has prayers we have yet to hear, let alone understand.

MEDITATION 308

Medicine wheel:
Compassion and empathy are evidence of love shared.

MEDITATION 309

Spiritual growth. At this moment, you are the sum total of every version of you.

MEDITATION 310

Natural law:
Compassion for Mother Earth creates
compassion for ourselves.

MEDITATION 311

Medicine wheel teaching:
Helping others is natural law. The foliage in the fall that drops from the tree allows for the new growth in the spring.

MEDITATION 312

Medicine wheel teaching,
Sacred Listening:
The future generations are consistently reaching out and speaking to us and trying to teach us.

MEDITATION 313

Mother Earth teaching:
Tuning in to the medicine. Sacred listening includes focusing on the sounds of gentleness and serenity.

MEDITATION 314

Unity.
Many tribes, one Creator. Many Nations, one Creator.
Many stars, one Creator.

MEDITATION 315

Natural law, Happiness:
If our lives do not include lifting each other up,
we will not find happiness.

MEDITATION 316

Two things we cannot replace:
time or healing.

MEDITATION 317

Natural law:
Sharing is connection. Connection is life.

MEDITATION 318

Spring Medicine, Natural law:
Like the flower, true abundance blooms from the inside.

MEDITATION 319

Turtles do not live in their shells. They are their shells. Humans do not live on Earth. We are Earth.

MEDITATION 320

Love Teaching:
Love is that spiritual place where the heart listens.

MEDITATION 321

Red Road:
Everything is the Red Road.

MEDITATION 322

The rebellious are asking for help.

MEDITATION 323

We have two businesses:
Help those people, places, and things that align with sacred law. Protect ourselves from those people, places, and things that are not aligned with sacred law.

MEDITATION 324

Spring medicine reclaims our own internal spring.

MEDITATION 325

Medicine Wheel teaching:
We are to rely on Mother Earth for all our healing.

MEDITATION 326

Sunrise medicine:
Rebirth is not a singular event but a prayerful healing and understanding that never leaves our hearts.

MEDITATION 327

Observation of medicine, Tree medicine:
We understand that some medicine is only found in the ground while other times it's found in the leaves. Some medicine is found in the Fall, while other medicine is located in the Spring.

MEDITATION 328

Creator, the ancestors, and the future generations did not bring us here to suffer but as an opportunity to create a good and better life. How we do this is part of our purpose, creating unity for all. This is how we find our place in the circle.

MEDITATION 329

Medicine Wheel:
Just as we are all related, so too are the medicines of Mother Earth. There is no hierarchy of medicine.
All are powerful and equal.

MEDITATION 330

Sacred Laws:
The Peacemakers are humility, love, truth, respect, honesty, strength, and wisdom.

MEDITATION 331

We decolonize our minds by shifting our relationship to Mother Earth and the Seven sacred teachings.

MEDITATION 332

Water has a Spirit. Water is life. We are water. Do you see the spirit of the water flowing inside you? How are you speaking to the water inside you? What are you offering the water inside you? Are you listening to the water inside you? Are you grateful for the water inside you?

MEDITATION 333

Eternal Spring. Our spiritual spring is waiting to bloom inside us all. We can begin at any time. This seed of love, part of the prayer of our ancestors that we are born with, is firmly planted when we are able to observe ourselves with peace and without judgment.

MEDITATION 334

If our prayers do not include our ancestors,
they are incomplete.

MEDITATION 335

Understanding our ancestral fires:
Our ancestral lands are rooted deep within our hearts. We cannot be separated. This connection is vital to understand our relationship with not only the rest of humanity but Mother Earth.

MEDITATION 336

The colonial world loves creating war, divisions, and being adversarial. Spiritual warfare versus simple connection. The simplicity of reclaiming Mother Earth and her ways isn't found on any battlefield with bombs and bullets but that soft, gentle place in the hearts and minds of the people.

MEDITATION 337

Gentle winds. One of our safe places should be our own voice. But are we sharing this safe place?

MEDITATION 338

The spiritual paradox is that the establishment of our individualism is found in our relationship with Mother Earth.

MEDITATION 339

Humanity cannot emotionally detox without Mother Earth. We cannot physically heal when separated from Mother Earth. We cannot be mentally stable without Mother Earth. We cannot spiritually align without Mother Earth.

MEDITATION 340

Wisdom:
The spiritual paradox is that we ascend spiritually by going within physically.

MEDITATION 341

Re-Earthing is remembering and walking with the ways of Earth.

MEDITATION 342

Transformation and growth. Until we change our prayers and our walk, our experiences always recycle.

MEDITATION 343

Breath and air. With every breath in, we get an opportunity to listen to our ancestors. Every breath out is an opportunity to offer gratitude to our ancestors.

MEDITATION 344

The things we offer, whether it's anger or kindness, reflect our spiritual abundance.

MEDITATION 345

We are Earth. Our natural spiritual navigation tools are water, fire, air, and Earth.

MEDITATION 346

Be wholeheartedly unapologetic in welcoming our new, very best version of ourselves.

MEDITATION 347

Life, like every season, not only has a beginning and an ending, but it also has spring, summer, fall, and winter. The lesson is learning to move through life with intent and grace.

MEDITATION 348

Medicine Wheel. East direction. East Medicine. Baby Medicine. We are supposed to connect to our childlike innocence, wonder, and curiosity through not just one season, but all.

MEDITATION 349

Our physical DNA reveals our spiritual ancestry.
This is not a place for colonial hierarchical thinking, rather a place of absolute celebration of life and the different spiritual fires we come from.

MEDITATION 350

Natural Law:
If we are stuck in one season, we will almost unknowingly resist seeing the medicine from all others. We have helpers and assistance in all seasons.

MEDITATION 351

Innocence and forgiveness have a beautiful and symbiotic relationship, both seen and unseen.
One cannot be whole without the other.

MEDITATION 352

Spiritual gifts:
Spring, summer, fall, and winter. Every new season holds a beautiful, unique gift for our individual growth.

MEDITATION 353

Sunrise offering:
What are we offering to our ancestors in return for another day of life?

MEDITATION 354

Spiritual circle medicine:
Every day understands the lessons of the previous day and assists the next. Every season understands the lessons of the last season and assists the next. Every year understands the lessons of the earlier years and helps in the next.

MEDITATION 355

Medicine Wheel teaching:
Every sunrise, day, season, and year has beautiful teachings waiting for us.

MEDITATION 356

Earth unity does not begin with the masses, nations, or religions. It begins spiritually with connecting to the one we cannot separate from: Mother Earth.

MEDITATION 357

True abundance begins with prayers, continues with gratitude, and ends with treating all life as sacred.

MEDITATION 358

We are Earth. We are the Medicine Wheel. We are connected to all seven directions. We all carry spring, summer, fall, and winter deep within us. We all carry fire, water, air, and Earth with us. We are the day. We are the night. We are the center of the universe. We are serenity. We are the ancestors. We are the future seven generations. We are the messengers of peace and the peacemakers.

MEDITATION 359

Abandoning our sacred seven laws (truth, love, humility, honesty, respect, courage, and wisdom) leaves us abandoned spiritually, emotionally, mentally, and physically.

MEDITATION 360

Our failures are a part of our experience. Learn from those experiences. We don't start over; we start with experience.

MEDITATION 361

Earth Medicine evolution:
Change the medicine and change our hearts. Change our hearts, change our world. Changing our world changes the future seven generations.

MEDITATION 362

The shift in our relationship with Mother Earth will look like a gentle battle from war to peace. Hate into love. Chaos into silence. Crisis into stillness.

MEDITATION 363

The celebration of life. The ceremony we seek is already around us, but the journey is to find it within us.

MEDITATION 364

Spring Medicine:
A time to revisit and reclaim our childlike innocence, vulnerability, wonder, and curiosity.

MEDITATION 365

We have to understand how powerful we are. Every prayer ripples out in every direction, forever.

About the Author

Wayne William Snellgrove, a Saulteaux Indian, was born on Fishing Lake First Nation Reserve in Saskatchewan. He is a modern-day genocide survivor of the Canadian government's policy of assimilation known as The 60s Scoop, a two-time USA National swimming champion and a USA Swimming National Team member. He is also the author of *Daily Medicine* and *Whispers from the Hollow Bone.*

www.ingramcontent.com/pod-product-compliance
Lightning Source LLC
Chambersburg PA
CBHW011213120626
46545CB00008B/2976

* 9 7 8 1 9 6 1 5 4 8 0 0 8 *